P9-BZF-208

THOMAS KINKADE

I'll Be Home for Christmas

Compiled by Anne Christian Buchanan

HARVEST HOUSE PUBLISHERS
Eugene, Oregon 97402

I'll Be Home for Christmas

Copyright © 1997 Thomas Kinkade, Media Arts Group, Inc., San Jose, CA
Published by Harvest House Publishers
Eugene, Oregon 97402

ISBN 1-56507-594-3

Manufactured in China

Design and production by:
Koechel Peterson & Associates, Minneapolis, Minnesota

98 99 00 01 02 03 04 05 06 /**NG**/ 10 9 8 7 6 5 4

Permissions and Acknowledgments
Page 3: "I'll Be Home for Christmas," words by Kim Gannon & music by
Walter Kent. Copyright © 1943, renewed © 1971. Reprinted with permission
of Gannon & Kent Music.
Page 32: Excerpt from "Grandma's House Held Christmas in Its Heart" by
May Traller. Copyright © 1944 The Des Moines Register and Tribune Company.
Reprinted with permission.
Page 35: Excerpt from *On the Banks of Plum Creek* by Laura Ingalls Wilder. Text
copyright © 1937 by Laura Ingalls Wilder, renewed © 1963 by Roger L.
MacBride. Reprinted with permission of HarperCollins Publishers.

Harvest House Publishers has made every effort to trace the ownership of
all poems and quotes. In the event of a question arising from the use of
a poem or quote, we regret any error made and will be pleased to make
the necessary correction in future editions of this book.

I'll Be
Home for
Christmas

I'll be home for Christmas.

You can plan on me.

Please have snow and mistletoe

And presents on the tree.

Christmas Eve will find me

Where the love light gleams.

I'll be home for Christmas,

If only in my dreams.

Kim Gannon

I shall attend to my little errands of love
    Early this year,

So that the brief days before Christmas may be
    Unhampered and clear

Of the fever of hurry. The breathless rushing
    That I have known in the past

Shall not possess me. I shall be calm in my soul
    And ready at last . . . .

I shall have leisure—I shall go out alone
    From my roof and my door;

I shall not miss the silver silence of stars
    As I have before;

And oh, perhaps—if I stand there very still
    And very long,

I shall hear what the clamor of living has kept from me—
    The angel's song.

Grace Noll Crowell

We inch up to Christmas—prepare, count days, keep secrets, watch for the signs. A red evening sky, every fleecy cloud on fire for a last few minutes before the winter night falls, still brings a shout, "Look! Christmas is coming! The angels are baking!"

Gertrud Mueller Nelson

Now and then, once in four or five years perhaps, the feathery snow lies a foot deep, fresh-fallen, on the still countryside and in the woods; and the waxing moon sheds her large light on all, and Nature holds her breath to wait for the happy day and tries to sleep, but cannot from sheer happiness and peace.

Indoors, the fire is glowing on the wide hearth, a great bed of coals that will last all night and be enough . . . and the older people sit round it, not saying much, and thinking with their hearts rather than with their heads, but small boys and girls know that interesting things have been happening in the kitchen all afternoon . . .

and the grown-ups and the children have made up any little differences of opinion they may have had, before supper time, because Good-Will must reign, and reign alone. . . . They are all happy in just waiting for King Christmas to open the door softly and make them all great people in his kingdom. But if it is the right sort of house, he is already looking in through the window, to be sure that everyone is all ready for him, and that nothing has been forgotten.

F. Marion Crawford

THE LITTLE CITY OF HOPE

Villagers all, this frosty tide,
Let your doors swing open wide,
Though wind may flow and snow betide
Yet draw us in by your fire to bide:
Joy shall be yours in the morning.

Here we stand in the cold
and the sleet,
Blowing fingers and stamping feet,
Come from far away, you to greet—
You by the fire and we in the street—
Bidding you joy in the morning.

For ere one half of the
night was gone,
Sudden a star has led us on,
Raining bliss and benison—
Bliss tomorrow and more anon,
Joy for every morning.

Good man Joseph toiled
  through the snow—
Saw the star o'er the stable low;
Mary she might not further go—
Welcome thatch and litter below!
Joy was hers in the morning.

━━◆◆◆━━

  And then they heard the angels tell,
  "Who were the first to cry Nowell?
  Animals all as it befell,
  In the stable where they did dwell!
  Joy shall be theirs in the morning."

Kenneth Grahame
THE WIND IN THE WILLOWS

"T his," said Mr. Pickwick, looking round him, "this is, indeed, comfort."

"Our invariable custom," replied Mr. Wardle. "Everybody sits down with us on Christmas eve, as you see them now—servants and all; and here we wait till the clock strikes twelve, to usher Christmas in, and wile away the time with forfeits and old stories. Trundle, my boy, rake up the fire."

"Come," said Wardle, "a song—a Christmas song."

Up flew the bright sparks in myriads as the logs were stirred, and the deep red blaze sent forth a rich glow, that penetrated into the furthest corner of the room, and cast its cheerful tint on every face.

"Come," said Wardle, "a song—a Christmas song."

Charles Dickens
THE PICKWICK PAPERS

hristmas Eve was Suzanne's own night. It had been made for her. Sitting on the floor with her back to the edge of the fireplace, arms around her knees while the light played over the room, she had that feeling which always came with this special night. She could not put it into words which satisfied her, but in some vague way knew it was magic—the night for which one lived all year.

In the summer, with the mourning doves and the bouncing-Bets, the wild grape-vine swings and the long walks in the timber, you forgot entirely the feeling that this night could bring. To think of it gave you no emotion whatever. In the early fall you began to remember it. By November it became a bright light toward which you walked. And now tonight you could not think with one bit of excitement how much you liked the summer things. Yes, it was magic. The snow piled against the window was not like other snows. The wind in the chimney was not like other winds. If you scratched a frosted place out of which to look, you saw that the snowpacked prairie to the north was a white country in which no other person lived, that the snowpacked timberland to the south was a white woods forever silent. It was as though there were no humans at all in any direction but your own family. Christmas Eve was a white light that drew a magic circle around the members of your own family to hem them all in and fasten them together.

Bess Streeter Aldrich

The door is on the latch tonight,
    The hearth-fire is aglow,
I seem to hear soft passing feet—
    The Christchild in the snow.

My heart is open wide tonight
    For stranger, kith or kin;
I would not bar a single door
    Where love might enter in.

AUTHOR UNKNOWN

And she brought forth her firstborn son, and wrapped
him in swaddling clothes, and laid him in a manger;
because there was no room for them in the inn.

THE GOSPEL OF LUKE

"hat's loving our neighbor better than ourselves, and I like it," said Meg, as they set out their presents while their mother was upstairs collecting clothes for the poor Hummels.

Not a very splendid show, but there was a great deal of love done up in the few little bundles, and the tall vase of red roses, white chrysanthemums, and trailing vines, which stood in the middle, gave quite an elegant air to the table.

"She's coming! Strike up, Beth! Open the door, Amy! Three cheers for Marmee!" cried Jo, prancing about while Meg went to conduct Mother to the seat of honor.

There were a good deal of laughing and kissing and explaining, in the simple, loving fashion which makes these home festivals so pleasant at the time, so sweet to remember long afterward.

Beth played her gayest march, Amy threw open the door, and Meg enacted escort with great dignity. Mrs. March was both surprised and touched, and smiled with her eyes full as she examined her presents and read the little notes which accompanied them. The slippers went on at once, a new handkerchief was slipped into her pocket, well scented with Amy's cologne, the rose was fastened in her bosom, and the nice gloves were pronounced a "perfect fit."

There were a good deal of laughing and kissing and explaining, in the simple, loving fashion which makes these home festivals so pleasant at the time, so sweet to remember long afterward.

Louisa May Alcott
LITTLE WOMEN

Joy to the World

Joy to the world! The Lord is come: Let earth receive her King;

Let ev'ry heart prepare Him room, and heav'n and nature sing,

And heav'n and nature sing, and heav'n, and heav'n and nature sing.

Joy to the world! The Saviour reigns: Let men their songs employ;

While fields and floods, rocks, hills and plains repeat the sounding joy,

Repeat the sounding joy, repeat, repeat the sounding joy.

He rules the world with truth and grace, and makes the nations prove

The glories of His righteousness, and wonders of His love,

And wonders of His love, and wonders, wonders of His love.

Isaac Watts

"A merry Christmas, a merry Christmas, a merry Christmas!" rang the Christmas bells across the snow.

Elfie kept her eyes shut tight, because she thought they were the fairy bells on the reindeer of Santa Claus; but Nancy sat up in bed and rubbed the sleep out of her eyes, and Pat suddenly gave a great shout. "It's Christmas Day!" he cried; and, just as he said this, Baby marched in at the door of the night nursery, beating his new drum, and after that there was no more sleep for anybody.

"Merry Christmasses, merry Christmasses!" shouted Baby, and he hammered mightily on his drum till Nurse came and took it away from him. . . .

"Why are the bells ringing like that?" said Elfie.

"Like what?" asked Nancy, who was still rubbing her eyes.

"As if they were laughing," said Elfie.

"I suppose they know it is Christmas Day," said Nancy.

"Bells do not laugh," said Nurse. "Bells ring."

"I think they laugh when they are Christmas bells," said Elfie.

Evelyn Sharp
THE CHILD'S CHRISTMAS

Christmas at Melrose

Come home with me a little space
And browse about our ancient place,
Lay by your wonted troubles here
And have a turn of Christmas cheer.
These sober walls of weathered stone
Can tell a romance of their own,
And these wide rooms of devious line
Are kindly meant in their design.
Sometimes the north wind searches through,
But he shall not be rude to you.
We'll light a log of generous girth
For winter comfort, and the mirth
Of healthy children you shall see
About a sparkling Christmas tree....
And you may chafe the wasting oak,
Or freely pass the kindly joke
To mix with nuts and home-made cake
And apples set on coals to bake.
Or some fine carol we will sing
In honor of the Manger-King....
These dear delights we fain would share
With friend and kinsman everywhere,
And from our door see them depart
Each with a little lighter heart.

Leslie Pinckney Hill

t last the dinner was all done, the cloth was cleared, the hearth swept, and the fire made up. The compound in the jug being tasted, and considered perfect, apples and oranges were put upon the table, and a shovelful of chestnuts on the fire. Then all the Cratchit family drew around the hearth in what Bob Cratchit called a circle, meaning half of one; and at Bob Cratchit's elbow stood the family display of glass. Two tumblers, and a custard-cup without a handle.

These held the hot stuff from the jug, however, as well as golden goblets would have done; and Bob served it out with beaming looks, while the chestnuts on the fire sputtered and cracked noisily. Then Bob proposed: "A Merry Christmas to us all, my dears. God bless us!" Which all the family re-echoed. "God bless us every one!" said Tiny Tim, last of all.

Charles Dickens
A CHRISTMAS CAROL

It was the policy of the good old gentleman to make his children feel that home was the happiest place in the world; and I value this delicious home-feeling as one of the choicest gifts a parent can bestow.

Washington Irving
CHRISTMAS EVE

his, then, is Christmas. Everything is silent in Dreamthorp. The smith's hammer reposes beside the anvil. The weaver's flying shuttle is at rest. Through the clear, wintry sunshine the bells this morning rang from the gray church tower amid the leafless elms, and up the walk the villagers trooped in their best dresses and their best faces....

Prayers over, the clergyman ... read out in that silvery voice of his, which is sweeter than any music to my ear, those chapters of the New Testament that deal with the birth of the Saviour. And the red-faced rustic congregation hung on the good man's voice as he spoke of the Infant brought forth in a manger, of the shining angels that appeared in the mid-air to the shepherds, of the miraculous star that took its station in the sky, and of the wise men who came from afar and laid their gifts of the frankincense and myrrh at the feet of the child. With the story every one was familiar, but on that day, and backed by the persuasive melody of the reader's voice it seemed to all quite new....

Alexander Smith

Sing a song of Christmas!
Pockets full of gold;
Plums and cakes for Polly's stocking,
More than it can hold.
Pudding in the great pot,
Turkey on the spit,
Merry faces round the fire,
Smiling quite a bit!
Sing a song of Christmas!
Carols in the street,
People going home with bundles
Everywhere we meet.
Holly, fir, and spruce boughs
Green upon the wall,
Spotless snow upon the road,
More about to fall.

AUTHOR UNKNOWN

ome houses are made for music and dancing. Others are built to hold life and love and mystery. Grandma's house was made for the purpose of holding Christmas in its heart forever.

You could catch the echo of Christmas carols from attic to cellar, and the fringe of icicles along the branches of the cedars just outside jingled like Christmas chime bells every time a wind danced by. The old house simply shouted of yuletide from rafter to corners. . . .

Soon we snuggled down. The fire snapped saucy fingers, the cedars brushed the windows, and the wind in the chimney hummed a Christmas anthem. I glanced up to where my stocking hung from the mantle, drowsiness swept over me, and I dreamed.

May Traller

**T**here had never been such a Christmas as this. It was such a large, rich Christmas, the whole church full of Christmas. There were so many lamps, so many people, so much noise and laughter, and so many happinesses in it. Laura felt full and bursting, as if that whole big rich Christmas were inside her, and her mittens and her beautiful jewelbox with the wee gold cup-and-saucer and teapot, and her candy and her popcorn ball. And suddenly someone said, "These are for you, Laura."

Mrs. Tower stood smiling, holding out the little fur cape and muff.

"For me?" Laura said, "For me?" Then everything else vanished while with both arms she hugged the soft furs to her....

"What do you say, Laura?" Ma asked, but the Reverend Alden said, "There is no need. The way her eyes are shining is enough...."

Laura Ingalls Wilder
ON THE BANKS OF PLUM CREEK

he little old country church looked very beautiful with its Christmas decorations. There were garlands of evergreens twined round the big stone pillars, and wreaths of holly hanging on all the pews, and bunches of red berries all along the top of the dark oak pulpit. And the sun shone in through the painted glass of the windows, and cast pretty red and blue and purple lights across everything, till Elfie began to think that the church must have been altered a little, on purpose, for Christmas Day. "I think the Christmas angel came down in the night and painted all those pretty colours, don't you?" she whispered to Bob, as they came out of church.

"You are a funny little girl, aren't you?" said Cousin Bob. But he did not laugh at her, and that was saying a good deal—for Cousin Bob.

THE CHILD'S CHRISTMAS

Happy, happy Christmas, that can win us back to the delusions of our childish days, that can recall to the old man the pleasures of his youth, that can transport the sailor and the traveller, thousands of miles away, back to his own fireside and his quiet home.

Charles Dickens
THE PICKWICK PAPERS

And I do come home at Christmas. We all do, or we all should. We all come home, or ought to come home, for a short holiday—the longer, the better....

Charles Dickens
A CHRISTMAS TREE

ow the season telescopes itself upon us. Christmas drops a plumb line down through the years! My father, a young man, sits at the end of the dining room table as we finish our Christmas morning breakfast, eating in desperation because we know we must—it is the family rule—before we go in together to our laden Christmas tree. My father leans forward. "I think I'd better go down to the office," he says. "You don't mind waiting an hour or two, do you?" It is part of the ritual, and we shriek our ritual protests. . . .

Moving back and forth from kitchen to dining room now, getting ready for supper, I looked into the living room at my own family circle—my husband, our four handsome teenaged children—and, for these few days, Hoyt's mother and father adding their special presence to our family scene. . . . Warmed, made content by all of this . . . I realized I was singing softly to myself. "We gather together to ask the Lord's blessing," I sang. I smiled—a Thanksgiving song and it's Christmas. I know why. But—*Joy to the world*, I thought. *Joy to the world!*

Martha Whitmore Hickman

O Father, may that Holy star
Grow every year more bright,
And send its glorious beams afar
To fill the world with light.

William Cullen Bryant

Christmas hath a darkness
      Brighter than the blazing noon,
Christmas hath a chillness
      Warmer than the heat of June,
Christmas hath a beauty
      Lovelier than the world can show:
For Christmas bringeth Jesus,
      Brought for us so low.

Earth, strike up your music,
      Birds that sing and bells that ring;
Heaven hath answering music
      For all Angels soon to sing:
Earth, put on your whitest
      Bridal robe of spotless snow:
For Christmas bringeth Jesus
      Brought for us so low.

Christina Rossetti

 **A**nd there were in the same country shepherds abiding in the field, keeping watch over their flock by night. And, lo, the angel of the Lord came upon them, and the glory of the Lord shone round them; and they were sore afraid.

And the angel said unto them, "Fear not; for behold, I bring you good tidings of great joy, which shall be to all people. For unto you is born this day in the city of David a Saviour, which is Christ the Lord. And this shall be a sign unto you: Ye shall find the babe wrapped in swaddling clothes, lying in a manger."

And suddenly there was with the angel a multitude of the heavenly host praising God, and saying, "Glory to God in the highest, and on earth peace, good will toward men."

And it came to pass, as the angels were gone away from them into heaven, the shepherds said one to another, "Let us now go even unto Bethlehem, and see this thing which is come to pass, which the Lord hath made known to us."

And they came with haste, and found Mary, and Joseph, and the babe lying in a manger.

The Gospel of Luke

I earnestly wish that every good brought into life by the Christmas Christ be yours, that you may have a heart of cheer, a spirit of hope, a life of love for every day in all the year.

George Eliot

Paintings